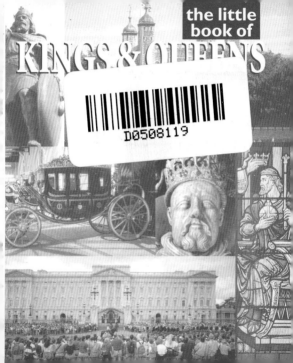

the little book of
KINGS & QUEENS

D0508119

Written and edited by Gill Knappett.
Designed by Tim Noel-Johnson.
Text and photographs © Jarrold Publishing.
The quotes on pp 82 and 85 are used by kind
permission of Buckingham Palace Press Office.

Publication in this form © Jarrold Publishing 2004,
latest reprint 2005.

Printed in China.
ISBN 0-7117-2997-2   2/05

Jarrold Publishing, Healey House, Dene Road, Andover,
Hampshire, SP10 2AA.
Tel: 01264 409200
e-mail: customer.services@jarrold-publishing.co.uk
website: www.britguides.com

Introduction

Since the rule of Alfred the Great in the 9th century to the present sovereign, Her Majesty Queen Elizabeth II, there have been 56 kings and queens of England – the mad, the sad, the good, the bad, the handsome and the ugly. Dip into over 100 fascinating facts, lovely legends and tragic tales about the men and women who have sat on the English throne in this imaginative 'timeline' of Britain's royal history.

The one and only

King Alfred, who ruled from 871–899, is the only ruler to have been given the tag 'Great'.

Can anyone smell burning?

The story of Alfred burning the cakes came about when, disguised as a traveller, he entered a Danish camp to spy on his enemies. A swineherd's wife left him to watch the cakes she was baking. The rest, as they say, is history.

The Alfred Jewel

The exquisite Alfred Jewel, a relic from the 9th century, bears the inscription 'Aelfred mec heht gewyrcan' (Alfred had me made). Discovered in 1693 at Newton Park, Somerset, this pear-shaped treasure – measuring approximately 6cm long by 4cm at its widest point – is now housed in the Ashmolean Museum, Oxford.

Edward and Aethelflaed

Edward the Elder, Alfred the Great's son who reigned 899–925, continued his father's work of maximizing Saxon rule and crushing Danish power. However, credit is equally due to his sister Aethelflaed – the formidable 'lady of Mercia' – who campaigned alongside Edward and assisted in defeating Danish settlers in the Midlands and East Anglia.

Rex Totius Britanniae

Edward's son, Athelstan, was one of the finest warriors to take the throne in medieval England. His victory at the Battle of Brunanburh in 937, defeating Irish, Scottish and Norse warlords, earned him the title *Rex Totius Britanniae* (King of all Britain).

Patron of the arts

As well as being a revered warrior, Athelstan was a great patron of the arts. An avid collector of carvings, jewels and precious metalwork, he was the first English king to be depicted on coins wearing a gold crown.

Edmund the Magnificent

Athelstan never married and his successor was his 18-year-old brother, Edmund. A popular man, Edmund's rule ended after only seven years when he was stabbed by Leof, an outlaw who tried to gatecrash a feast in the king's hall, Pucklechurch in Gloucestershire. When Edmund intervened in the ensuing argument, he was fatally wounded.

Vegetarian king

Edward the Elder's third son took the throne on Edmund's death. Edred was a sickly man, whose digestive system forced him to be vegetarian. However, his physical weakness did not deter him from a ruling style of strength and subtlety which enabled him to regain Saxon control of the whole northern kingdom.

Eadwig the Fair

Next in line to the throne on Edred's death at the age of 30 was the 13-year-old son of Edmund, Eadwig – a handsome man who died before he was 20.

First king of all England

At the age of just 12, Edgar was ruler of Mercia and Northumbria, becoming King of Wessex on his brother Eadwig's death in 959. On Whit Sunday 973 Edgar (known as Edgar the Peaceful) was crowned the first king of all England at the abbey church in Bath, in a ceremony on which all subsequent coronations have been based. A beautiful stained-glass window in Bath Abbey commemorates the event.

Wicked stepmother

Edgar's elder son, another Edward, succeeded his father in 975 when he was 13. Born to Edgar's first wife, he met with the hostility of his stepmother, who had designs on the Crown for Ethelred, the son she had borne Edgar. In 978 young Edward rode to Corfe in Dorset where Ethelred's supporters crowded him in mock welcome and stabbed him to death.

Edward the Martyr

Following his early demise, Edward was hastily buried in Wareham but reinterred the following year in the royal mausoleum at Shaftesbury. It was whispered that the body had not decayed; other tales tell that parts of the skeleton were stolen as holy relics, and miracles attributed to them. Whatever the reality, Ethelred – feeling some guilt in the proceedings surrounding Edward's murder – had his half-brother canonized as Edward the Martyr.

Ethelred Unraed

Edward's successor was Ethelred Unraed ('unraed' meaning 'no reputable policy') though his name is now often corrupted to Ethelred the Unready. He reigned for 37 years but lost all that his predecessors had achieved against the Danes.

Forkbeard v. the Unready

By 1013, Ethelred's greatest enemy, Swein, King of Denmark (known as Forkbeard), had overrun the country and Ethelred fled to Normandy. He returned in 1014 on Swein's death, and ruled again for a short period.

Edmund Ironside

Edmund Ironside, son of Ethelred and so-called because of his physical strength, enjoyed a short but acclaimed reign, during which time he staged many successful battles against the Danes and cleared the south of England of the enemy in a few months. Crowned at Old St Paul's Cathedral, he died at Oxford in 1016: some reports say he was assassinated, possibly by disembowelling; others say he was exhausted and in ill-health following a serious wound received at a last, unsuccessful battle where the Saxons were slaughtered.

Cnut and the waves

On the death of Edmund Ironside, Cnut, the son of Swein of Denmark, became King of Denmark, Norway and England, as well as overlord of Scotland. He is famous for the incident where, in an effort to stop the unwelcome flattery of his courtiers, he made them sit by the sea and watch while the incoming tide disobeyed his command to retreat.

Harold Harefoot

The heir to Cnut's throne in England was Harthacnut, his son by his second – and official – wife in England. However, Harthacnut (King of Denmark) was involved in a power struggle with the King of Norway and, while he was otherwise occupied, Harold (nicknamed Harefoot), Cnut's older son by a previous wife, claimed the throne and ruled for five years.

Harthacnut's half-brotherly love

When Harold died his half-brother, Harthacnut, took the Crown and had Harold's body flung into a marsh.

Edward the Confessor

England's royal link with Denmark ceased on Harthacnut's death and the throne passed to Edward, Ethelred Unraed's surviving son. The pious Edward took great interest in religion and instructed the rebuilding of Westminster Abbey, which was consecrated on 28 December 1065. He died a few days later, on 5 January 1066, and was canonized in 1161.

Harold and Hastings

Edward failed to produce an heir, so the Crown passed to a man chosen by the nobles and, it is said, by Edward himself on his deathbed – Harold, son of Earl Godwin. Although famous for his victory over the Norwegians at Stamford Bridge, Harold is perhaps best remembered for his death at the Battle of Hastings in 1066.

One in the eye

Contrary to popular belief, the Bayeux Tapestry shows King Harold being felled by a sword – it was some other chap nearby who got the arrow in the eye.

Do you come here often?

Following his victory over Harold, William the Conqueror was crowned in Westminster Abbey on Christmas Day 1066. Records show only four visits to England by King William between 1072 and his death in 1087.

Domesday Book

William I's last visit to England's shores in 1085 saw his instigation of the survey that was to be recorded as the Domesday Book, so-called because no one could contest its findings – just like the Day of Judgement, or Doom.

Ouch!

King William is said to have died a painful death from peritonitis, following an accident with the pommel of a saddle when his horse stumbled.

Rosy-cheeked king

William Rufus – the second son of William I who claimed the throne on his death – was so-called because of his ruddy complexion.

A dastardly deed?

Was William Rufus's death an accident? His younger brother, Henry, was at the hunting party where William met his fate. Henry immediately rode to Winchester to secure the royal treasury, and was hugely generous to the family of the man who shot the fatal arrow. He was crowned four days after his brother died.

First zoo

Henry I took a great interest in exotic animals from abroad and established the first zoo in England.

Something fishy

Henry I had three legitimate children: one boy died in infancy, another tragically drowned, and he married off his daughter to the German Emperor Henry V. Henry's own death followed a feast in France where, after consuming a large number of lampreys (eel-like fish which his doctors had forbidden him to eat), he contracted ptomaine poisoning.

Empress escapes

It was Henry's nephew, Stephen, who next took the Crown. Henry's daughter, the Empress Matilda, now married to the Count of Anjou, challenged his right to the throne. In 1142 she was held captive in Oxford Castle but escaped across the ice-covered river during a snowstorm, camouflaged in a white sheet.

King's Day and Saint's Day

The coronation of King Stephen took place in 1135 on 26 December – St Stephen's Day. St Stephen was the first Christian martyr and, fittingly, his death is celebrated the day after the birth of Christ.

Haute couture

King Stephen's son, Eustace, predeceased his father and the sovereignty passed to the Empress Matilda's son, Henry II. He was nicknamed Henry Curtmantle because of the short style of cloak he wore, a French fashion quite different to the long cloaks worn in England.

St Thomas Becket

Following disputes with his former friend, Thomas Becket (Archbishop of Canterbury), four of Henry II's knights overheard the king mutter, 'Will no one rid me of this turbulent priest?' In an attempt to please their sovereign, the knights murdered Becket in his own cathedral on 29 December 1170. Becket was canonized and Canterbury Cathedral became a site of Christian pilgrimage.

Richard Lionheart

Commemorated with a statue outside the Houses of Parliament, Richard I, son

of Henry II, spent less time in England than any king before or since. His skill and courage in battle earned him the title *Cœur De Lion* (heart of the lion).

Magna Carta

King John, Richard I's brother and successor, is perhaps best remembered for putting his seal to the document that became known as Magna Carta (or Great Charter, the 'cornerstone of English liberties') at Runnymede, near Windsor, on 15 June 1215.

Lost in the Wash

Legend has it that King John lost his crown and other valuables when crossing the Wellstream which flowed into the Wash, now an irresistible magnet for treasure hunters. The King John Cup, thought to be part of his treasure, is housed in the Guildhall in King's Lynn.

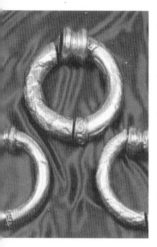

Junior king

King John's first-born acceded to the throne in 1216 as Henry III at nine years old. He was hastily crowned in Gloucester Cathedral with a gold torque or bracelet, the state crown having been lost in the Wash, and again in 1220 at Westminster Abbey with full ceremony.

Confessing admiration

Henry III held one of his ancient predecessors, Edward the Confessor, in great reverence, naming his first-born after him and rebuilding his abbey at Westminster where he had Edward's relics reinterred in a magnificent new shrine.

Edward Longshanks

Exceptionally tall and handsome, Henry III's heir, Edward I, was known as Edward Longshanks. Although given the official title King Edward I, there had already been three previous Edwards on the English throne.

Princes of Wales

It was during Edward I's reign that the principality of Wales came under English rule, and in a symbolic gesture he proclaimed his baby son, born at Caernarfon, Prince of Wales. Prince Charles, current heir to the throne, is the 21st holder of the Prince of Wales title; his investiture took place at Caernarfon Castle on 1 July 1969.

Stone of Scone goes home

Despite his success in Wales, Edward I was unable to assert his powers over Scotland, though his relentless attempts earned him the title 'Hammer of the Scots'. During one campaign, Edward captured the Stone of Scone on which all Scottish kings had been crowned. Subsequently the chair made to house the stone has seated all but three future kings and queens of England at their coronations in Westminster Abbey, including Queen Elizabeth II. In 1996 the trophy was returned to Scotland on, fittingly, St Andrew's Day (30 November).

Three Edwards

Edward I's successor and namesake, Edward II, his 13th child and only son by his first wife to survive childhood, was a tall and handsome man like his father, but a weak ruler and soldier. His defeat by Robert the Bruce at the Battle of Bannockburn in 1314 secured Scottish independence for another 300 years. His French queen, Isabella, played a part in his deposition in favour of their son, also Edward. Edward II died a grisly, tortured death at Berkeley Castle in Gloucestershire in 1327 and is buried in Gloucester Cathedral.

Order of the Knights of the Garter

Controlled by his mother and her lover in his early years, Edward III finally asserted himself: the lover was executed; his mother was retired to Castle Rising in Norfolk. In 1348 he founded the Order of the Knights of the Garter (inspired by King Arthur and his Knights of the Round Table) as the highest honour bestowed by the king on 26 knights for loyalty and military merit. The tradition continues today when, each June, new knights are invested at Windsor Castle.

What happened to Wat?

Edward III's heir would have been his son Edward, the Black Prince, but he predeceased his father and the Crown passed to the late prince's ten-year-old son, Richard. At just 14, Richard II faced

the challenge of the Peasants' Revolt and famously calmed a dangerous mob at Smithfield, during which incident Wat Tyler, the rebel's spokesman, was killed.

Starved or murdered?

In 1399 Richard II was forced to abdicate in favour of his cousin, Henry IV. Richard died the following year – possibly by self-starvation, possibly murdered – while imprisoned at Pontefract Castle.

English through and through

Henry IV was the first king to be born in England of English parents since the reign of William the Conqueror.

Death in Jerusalem

It was prophesied that Henry IV would die in Jerusalem and, in a way, he did – breathing his last in Westminster Abbey's Jerusalem Chamber after suffering a seizure while at prayer.

Mad father-in-law

Henry IV's son, Henry V, achieved what many had set out to do – conquer France. Two incidents stand out: his great victory at Agincourt in 1415, where English archers destroyed the French troops; and the Treaty of Troyes in 1420, where Henry was recognized as heir and Regent of France, taking Catherine of Valois, daughter of the mad King Charles VI of France, as his wife.

The youngest king

Henry VI – the youngest English sovereign – was not yet one year old when he acceded to the throne on the death of his father.

From Eton to Cambridge

In 1441 King Henry VI laid the foundation stone of King's College, Cambridge, built to house twelve scholars from his newly established Eton College, near Windsor. For over 400 years King's only admitted Etonians and it was not until 1873 that the tradition changed.

A sad life

During his lifetime Henry VI suffered bouts of insanity, was dominated by bullying members of Court and a formidable wife, saw civil war in the shape of the Wars of the Roses, was imprisoned, deposed and restored to the throne, received an arrow wound in the neck, saw his only child predecease him, and was eventually murdered in the Tower of London.

A protector, his son and a king undone

The son of Richard, Duke of York, claimed the throne twice as Edward IV – from 1461–70 during Henry VI's deposition and again on his death in 1471. Richard had himself governed the country as Protector when Henry suffered his first bout of madness, and his continued bid for power led to the Wars of the Roses, during which he was killed.

York overlooks York

In medieval times it was customary for the severed heads of traitors to be displayed at York's Micklegate Bar, the main entrance into the city from the south and the most important as it was used by England's monarchs. Following Richard of York's defeat at Wakefield in 1460, his head – adorned with paper crown – was exhibited, an event which inspired William Shakespeare's later witticism:

Off with his head, and set it on York gates;
So York may overlook the town of York.

Henry VI Part 3, Act I, Scene iv

The Princes in the Tower

On Edward IV's death in 1483 his young son ascended the throne as Edward V, but his reign was to be short. The dead king's brother, Richard of Gloucester, was

protector of the realm; under his instruction – and desire to take the Crown for himself – the boy king and his brother, Richard of York, mysteriously disappeared into the Tower of London and were never seen alive again.

Hunchback of Gloucester

Following the disappearance of his nephews in 1483, Richard of Gloucester became King Richard III. Although often depicted as a hunchback, he probably only had one shoulder higher than the other.

Under the hawthorn bush

Richard III reigned for just two years. He was the last English monarch to die in battle, killed at the Battle of Bosworth Field where his crown rolled under a hawthorn bush; the story goes that Lord Stanley retrieved it and placed it on the head of the battle's victor, Henry Tudor.

Keeping it in the family

The warring houses of York and Lancaster were united when Henry VII (Henry Tudor) married Elizabeth of York, the eldest daughter of Edward IV and sister of the Princes in the Tower. Henry was proud of his Welsh ancestry and believed that he was related to the legendary King Arthur, after whom he named his first born. But Prince Arthur was doomed never to become king, dying less than six months after marrying Catherine of Aragon, later the queen of his brother Henry VIII.

Six weddings and a dissolution

Henry VIII is best known for marrying six wives, but is also famous for founding the Church of England and the dissolution of the monasteries – a result of his break with Rome when the Pope refused to give his blessing for the annulment of Henry's marriage to Catherine of Aragon on her failure to provide him with a male heir.

Six wives' fates

'Divorced, beheaded, died,
Divorced, beheaded, survived.'
So goes the rhyme which records in
turn the fate of Henry VIII's six wives:
Catherine of Aragon, Anne Boleyn,
Jane Seymour, Anne of Cleves,
Catherine Howard and Catherine Parr.

Henry's hobbies

Henry VIII was a fine scholar and musician,
whose compositions include *Pastime with
Good Company*. The melody *Greensleeves* is
often attributed to him, though there is
no evidence that he penned it.

Fickle finger of fashion

Henry VIII's second wife, Anne Boleyn, had six fingers on her left hand – a medical condition known as polydactyly – and legend has it that she engineered a

change in the style of fashion for sleeves in order to conceal her extra digit. Anne's enemies claimed her additional finger was a sign that she was a witch – an excuse Henry used, along with her alleged infidelity, to have her executed.

Grammar school boy

Edward VI was Henry VIII's longed-for son, born at Hampton Court in 1537 to his third wife, Jane Seymour, who died a few days after the birth. Jane was the king's best-loved wife, having succeeded where all his other wives failed in producing a male heir. Henry was buried next to her in St George's Chapel at Windsor Castle when he died, leaving Edward, a sickly nine-year-old, as king. Although Edward only lived to the age of 15, he loved learning and is remembered for founding many grammar schools bearing his name.

Nine-days queen

The Duke of Northumberland persuaded the dying Edward VI to choose the king's cousin – and Northumberland's daughter-in-law – Lady Jane Grey as his heiress. The reluctant girl was proclaimed queen on 10 July 1553, four days after Edward passed away. But the supporters of Mary, Henry VIII's daughter by Catherine of Aragon, rose in protest and just nine days later, on 19 July 1553, Jane was taken to the Tower of London and held prisoner. She was beheaded there in February 1554, aged 16.

Bloody Mary

Mary was declared illegitimate by her father, Henry VIII, when he had his marriage to Catherine of Aragon annulled. But Mary took the Crown on her young half-brother's death, having seen off her unfortunate rival, Lady Jane Grey. Mary I's efforts to eradicate Protestantism resulted in the execution of many who followed that faith, including the Oxford Martyrs: Protestant leaders Archbishop Cranmer, Bishop Ridley and Bishop Latimer. They were burned at the stake in Oxford and are commemorated by a memorial there.

Gloriana

Mary was childless when she died, and Elizabeth, Mary's half-sister and daughter of Henry and Anne Boleyn, took her place as queen. Elizabeth I was popular with her subjects but the high point of her reign was Drake's defeat of the Spanish Armada in 1588. As a result of this achievement the nation basked in its elevated status and glory, and affectionately dubbed its queen 'Gloriana'.

The virgin and the frog

Virginia in the USA is named after Elizabeth, the Virgin Queen. Probably a virgin when she died, during her lifetime she had many suitors; the one who is said to have been closest to winning her hand was Hercules-François, Duke of Alençon, whom she endearingly called 'my little frog'.

National anthem

It was Elizabeth I's organist, John Bull, who composed *God Save the Queen*.

Elizabeth and Mary

Mary Queen of Scots' grandmother was Henry VIII's only sister. Those who did not recognize the annulment of his marriage to Catherine of Aragon declared Elizabeth, the product of his second marriage, illegitimate and Mary the rightful heir to the English throne. Elizabeth's insecurity in the matter led, in part, to her reluctantly consenting to Mary's imprisonment and eventual execution.

More than one name

After a 44-year rule, the sovereignty passed, with the dying Queen Elizabeth's blessing, to the son of Mary Queen of Scots in 1603. James VI of Scotland, who became James I of England, had been baptized Charles James – the first British monarch to be given more than one Christian name.

King's speech

As well as inheriting his father's Crown, Charles, the only surviving son of James I, had the misfortune to inherit his speech impediment.

Charles and his two shirts

Like his father before him, Charles I faced problems with Parliament, culminating in the Civil War between Cavaliers and

Roundheads. When the Royalist troops finally fell, Charles was imprisoned and eventually sentenced to death. On the day of his execution he wore two shirts, for the weather was cold and he was concerned that the people watching would think he shook with fear.

Haunting hooves

For four years during the Civil War, Charles I made the city of Oxford his capital; Royalist forces gathered in New College Lane before going to battle and the street is said to echo with the sound of ghostly horses' hooves.

Popular name

Charles I named his first-born Charles. Sadly, the baby died at birth, and the king gave his second son – who was to become Charles II – the same name.

Royal Oak

Many public houses are named the Royal Oak after an incident during the Civil War, when Charles II suffered defeat at the hands of Cromwell's army at the Battle of Worcester in 1651. A £1,000 reward was offered for the king's capture, and he was on the run for six weeks – during which time he allegedly spent 14 hours hiding in an oak tree at Boscobel in Shropshire. An oak tree there is said to have grown from an acorn of the original tree, planted in exactly the same spot.

London's burning

Charles II's reign was to encounter both the Great Plague of London in 1665 and the Great Fire the following year. The fire started at the premises of the king's baker, Thomas Farynor, in Pudding Lane – today the site of the Monument. Charles is reputed to have helped put out the flames; other tales tell of him supervising the demolition of houses to create an open area that the fire would be unable to cross.

How's your father?

Nell Gwynne was Charles II's most famous mistress but he sired many offspring by numerous others. His marriage to Catherine of Braganza, daughter of the King of Portugal, was childless and none of his illegitimate children could be his successor – that role fell to his younger brother, James. But because of his strong Catholic leanings, many favoured James's daughter Mary (married to her cousin, William, Prince of Orange) to become sovereign.

Exiled king

With his commitment to the Roman Church, James II was eager to convert England to Catholicism but found few supporters. Several lords and bishops collaborated and invited James's nephew and son-in-law, the Prince of Orange, to intervene. Prince William's subsequent invasion to safeguard the Protestant interest was successful. James escaped to France and Parliament declared he had abdicated on 11 December 1688. Despite attempts and plans to regain the throne, James never succeeded and died, exiled in France, in 1701.

William ♥ Mary

Mary, eldest daughter of James II, was the first to be given the title Princess Royal. She was just eight years old when she first met her cousin William, nearly 12 years her senior, the man who was to become her husband. When told she was to marry a foreigner, Mary is said to have cried for two days. However, the joint monarchs, crowned at Westminster Abbey on 11 April 1689, were a devoted couple who enjoyed a happy marriage.

Money matters

During William and Mary's reign, Lloyds insurance office opened in London and the Bank of England was established.

Toasted mole

After Mary's death from smallpox in 1694, William reigned alone. He died in 1702 after complications set in following a fall from his horse. William's mount had apparently stumbled on a molehill and Jacobites everywhere raised their glasses 'to the little gentleman in the black velvet' who brought about the demise of their enemy.

Blenheim Palace

William and Mary had no children and Mary's sister Anne became queen when William died. Her one-time great friend and confidante was Sarah, wife of John Churchill, first Duke of Marlborough, whose great victory at the Battle of Blenheim in 1704 led to the queen gifting to him the grounds of what became the Blenheim Palace estate.

Queen Anne's legs

The elegant style of furniture known as Queen Anne, particularly distinctive for its cabriole legs, was so named because it became popular during her reign.

Not the king's English

Although she had 17 pregnancies, the only child of Queen Anne to survive infancy was a son, William – but sadly he died aged 11. On Anne's death the English throne fell to her second cousin, the Elector of Hanover, who became George I. He spent as little time in England as possible and it is generally believed that he spoke no English.

Another slice of melon, George?

George I died after a stroke brought on by gorging himself on too much melon when he was insufficiently recovered from a bout of seasickness. He was succeeded by his son, also George.

Bainting and boetry

Although fluent in English, George II never lost his guttural German accent. He was a great patron of music – Handel's *Water Music* is thought to have been composed for him – but otherwise disliked the arts and said he could not stand 'bainting and boetry'.

Love you too, mum

The eldest son of George II and his queen, Caroline, was Prince Frederick, who was on bad terms with his parents.

The queen reputedly said of her son: 'My dear first-born is the greatest ass, the greatest liar and the greatest beast in the whole world and I heartily wish he was out of it.'

Kew Gardens

The original 'botanick garden' at Kew was founded in 1759 by George II's daughter-in-law, Augusta, Dowager Princess of Wales.

Mad Farmer George

Prince Frederick predeceased his father, and the Crown passed to his brother George – the first English monarch from the House of Hanover to be born and bred in England. George III, nicknamed 'Farmer George' for his love of agriculture, suffered a genetic and progressively worsening mental illness known as porphyria and died insane.

Buck House bargain

George III bought Buckingham House, now Buckingham Palace, in 1762 for the sum £28,000.

I do like to be beside the seaside …

George III's son was the fourth consecutive George to take the throne. As Prince Regent he displayed flamboyant tastes, perhaps best portrayed in his breathtakingly ornate Royal Pavilion in Brighton. Brighton, previously a fishing village, became a fashionable seaside resort as a result of the king's regular visits.

Silly Billy the Sailor King

George IV's only child, Princess Charlotte, died in 1817 after a difficult labour. On the king's death in 1830, his brother William acceded to the throne. William IV had two nicknames – 'the Sailor King', because of his career in the navy which he entered when he was 13, and 'Silly Billy' for his lack of intellect and tact.

Long to reign over us

William IV had no surviving children and his niece, Victoria, took the Crown at just 18. One of the most revered of Britain's monarchs, she reigned for 63 years.

Missed again

Queen Victoria was not popular with everyone – she survived eight assassination attempts between 1840 and 1882.

For valour

The most senior military decoration, the Victoria Cross, was introduced in 1856.

Christmas decorations

The custom of decorating an evergreen tree at Christmas was popularized in England when Prince Albert, Queen Victoria's German-born consort, remembering the tradition from his childhood, decorated a large tree in Windsor Castle to entertain the couple's nine children.

Official birthday

Queen Victoria is said to have instigated the sovereign's 'official birthday' because her own fell on 24 May when she was usually at Balmoral. Her son, Edward VII, whose birthday was in November, formalized the day to be marked June, in the hope of good weather. The tradition continues to this day when Queen Elizabeth II celebrates the event on a Saturday in June with the annual Trooping the Colour, more correctly known as the Sovereign's Birthday Parade, during which ceremony she inspects her personal troops on Horse Guards Parade.

A widow's weeds

When Queen Victoria's beloved husband died aged 42, she was devastated and withdrew from the public eye for 13 years. Her prolonged isolation led to a campaign to abolish the monarchy, and the Prime Minister, Benjamin Disraeli, finally enticed her back into public life. But she dressed in funereal black until her death in 1901.

We are amused

One of Queen Victoria's granddaughters, Princess Alice, when interviewed on television, announced that the queen had once told her she had never uttered the phrase 'We are not amused'.

Together forever

Victoria and Albert are buried together in the Royal Mausoleum which she had built at Frogmore, Windsor. Above the mausoleum door is inscribed: 'Farewell best beloved, here at last I shall rest with thee, with thee in Christ I shall rise again'.

Good-time Bertie

By the time Queen Victoria died, her son and heir was already a grandfather. Despite being reared by parents with high moral standards, Edward VII lived a hedonistic lifestyle: he enjoyed sports, especially horse racing, and loved motor cars, good food, cigars, the theatre – and women. His mother believed that the scandal of his alleged affair with an actress hastened his father's death.

Post-dated coronation

A few days before his coronation, arranged for 26 June 1902, an emergency operation was carried out on Edward VII for acute appendicitis. The ceremony was postponed until 9 August that year, but many souvenirs commemorating the event carry the original date.

Royal retreat

Edward VII bought the Sandringham Estate in Norfolk in 1862. Sandringham House, built in 1870, remains a popular retreat for today's Royal Family, especially at Christmas.

House of Windsor

Edward VII's eldest son, Albert, died aged 28 so it was his second son, George, who ascended the throne when his father passed away. George V's reign was overshadowed by the First World War and, as a result of the anti-German feelings of British people at the time, he changed his family name from Saxe-Coburg-Gotha to Windsor on 17 July 1917. In 1960, Queen Elizabeth II changed it again, to Mountbatten-Windsor.

In memoriam

To commemorate those who died during the First World War, George V unveiled the Cenotaph in Whitehall, London, in 1920. The word 'cenotaph' is derived from the Greek for 'empty tomb'.

King and Kipling's Christmas message

In 1932 George V became the first monarch to broadcast a Christmas Day message to the nation via the wireless. Reading from a script written by the author Rudyard Kipling, the king said: 'I speak now from my home and from my heart to you all; to men and women so cut off by the snows, the desert, or the sea, that only voices out of the air can reach them.'

How rude!

Following a serious illness, George V convalesced at Craigwell House near Bognor. It is unlikely that the king enjoyed his stay for during a subsequent relapse when it was suggested he go there again, he refused with, allegedly, the oft-quoted words 'B***** Bognor!'

For the love of Wallis

Following George V's death his vain but charming eldest son David acceded the throne on 20 January 1936 as Edward VIII. But he was never crowned. He abdicated – the only British monarch to do so voluntarily – for the love of divorcée Wallis Simpson after reigning for just 325 days.

CH

Abdication speech

Edward VIII's abdication speech was written with the help of Winston Churchill. Broadcast on the radio on 11 December 1936, it famously included the words: 'I have found it impossible to carry on the heavy burden of responsibility and to discharge the duties of king as I would wish to do without the help and support of the woman I love.'

Reluctant king

On Edward VIII's abdication his younger
brother, Albert (Bertie), became King
George VI, a role he had never expected
or wanted, and granted his predecessor
the title Duke of Windsor. Bertie had
been a sickly child, lacked his brother's
natural charisma, and had a stammer
which didn't help his shy manner – but he
was a brave and conscientious leader.
Although he was dogged by illness during
his adult life, his queen, Elizabeth, the
Queen Mother, always blamed his early
death on the pressure imposed on him as
a result of his brother's abdication.

Same date, different brother

George VI's coronation took place on 12 May 1937, the day his brother should have been crowned.

Buckingham bombed

In September 1940, two bombs fell on Buckingham Palace – the worst of nine hits it was to receive during the Second World War. Queen Elizabeth, consort

of George VI, who had refused to take her family abroad for the duration of the war to show its support for the nation, is reported to have said she was glad they had been bombed because: 'It makes me feel we can look the East End in the face.'

Grease monkey princess

During the Second World War the heir to the throne, George VI's elder daughter, Princess Elizabeth, joined the Auxiliary Transport Service and trained as a driver and mechanic.

Like a queen

On 6 February 1952, Princess Elizabeth was in Kenya at the start of a world tour when the news of her father's sudden death was brought to her. When an aide, Major Charteris, was asked at a press conference how she had taken the news, he replied, 'Bravely, like a queen.'

What's on telly?

Elizabeth II's coronation was the first televised event of such magnitude. The government did not want television cameras inside Westminster Abbey but The Queen overruled the decision.

The Queen's Coronation Day

THE PICTORIAL RECORD OF THE HISTORIC OCCASION

On the box

On 2 June 1953 an estimated 20 million viewers saw Queen Elizabeth II being crowned, including those watching large screens in cinemas, church halls and hospitals, and those invited to view the televisions of lucky neighbours who had a set. The broadcast heralded a dramatic increase in the purchase of television sets which were a rare luxury in those days, and indeed it was the first time many people had ever watched 'the box'.

And another thing ...

On Elizabeth II's Coronation Day, it was announced that Edmund Hillary and Tenzing Norgay had conquered Mount Everest, the world's highest mountain.

It's a dog's life

The Queen is well-known for her fondness of dogs, especially corgis; the first one she owned was named Dookie. As a result of the royal corgis mixing with the family dachshunds, there have been quite a few royal 'Dorgis'.

Have you any ID?

At the State Opening of Parliament, which takes place each November, The Queen arrives in the Irish State Coach, passing through Horse Guards Arch, a thoroughfare through which only the blue-blooded are permitted to ride.